Learn 2 Think

All About Me
Journal for kids

A journal to preserve kids memories and cherish them for a lifetime!

New Edition 2014
Copyright Learn 2 Think Pte Ltd

Email: contactus@learn-2-think.com

ALL RIGHTS RESERVED. No part of this publication may be reproduced, stored in a retrieval system or transmitted in any form or by any means, electronic, mechanical or photocopying, recording or otherwise, without prior written permission of the publishers.

This book is designed to provide information in regard to the subject matter covered. The contents of this book are for educational purposes only. Although every precaution has been taken in the preparation of this book, the publisher and author assume no responsibility for errors or omissions. The authors have made all reasonable efforts to provide current and accurate information for the readers of this book. The authors cannot be held liable for any unintentional errors or omissions that may be found. Please not that all text, images, graphics used in the book are a copyright of Learn 2 Think Pte. Ltd. Wherever the information, products, services or items have originated from a third party, every effort has been made to credit the original creator. In case of an accidental omission, please contact us and we will credit your attributes or remove the item.

ISBN-13:

978-1484977699

Intro

All About Me journal is full of thought provoking questions on each page that will invite children to take a deeper look at themselves and things around them. A thought prompt may ask them to describe their father's job or make a list of things they wish for their family, describe their school to a stranger or write about what gets them upset, recall their favorite childhood toy or pen down a thank you note to a friend who once helped them. This journal has it all that will make children delighted each time they write it.

All this journal needs is a pen and children's thoughts to turn it into a magical gift that will never stop giving.

Happy Journaling!

A Special Note for Kids:

This journal is specially for you 'coz you are a special one and so is every thought sitting in every corner of your mind. This journal has been designed to record your precious thoughts and turn them into memories that you can turn back to and remember any time in future. As you record your achievements and triumphs, your concerns and worries, special moments and everyday moments, your feelings and opinions you would preserve your memories for a lifetime.

All About Me journal is full of thought provoking questions on each page that will invite you to take a deeper look at yourself and things around you. A thought prompt may ask you to describe your father's job or make a list of things you wish for your family, describe your school to a stranger or write about what gets you upset, recall your favorite childhood toy or pen down a thank you note to a friend who once helped you. This journal has it all that will make you delighted each time you write it.

All it needs is a pen and you to turn it into a magical gift that will never stop giving.

Note to Parents

The habit of writing a journal helps children to disentangle their thoughts and ideas and connects their inner thinking with actual events of life. Reflecting and recording thoughts helps children to become more aware of their beliefs, ideas, opinions and experiences. It gets them alive to discover themselves as thinking individuals. It is a great practice to engage in the process of deep thinking and analysis to pen down thoughts on experiences that life offers!

All About Me journal will be a great learning experience for your child that will give a very creative engagement to the child's brain to yield a creative output. It will encourage clarity of thinking and expressing. At a more practical level, it will train your child to summarize and report events, organize information and come up with a structured writing.

This is a perfect journal for your child and an inviting way to encourage them to reflect on their life and begin writing down their thoughts and feelings in their own words. Upon completing the journal it can be a valuable keepsake for kids; something they can look back on as an adult.

Few questions that usually concern many parents about journaling are: When and where should journal writing take place? How often should one write? What is a good time to write? The answer is to write as often as your child can. The real benefits of journal writing start showing over a period of time with sustained writing. So develop a routine for your child when they can turn on to this journal in a preferably quite setting where your child can concentrate and listen to his/her inner self. The reflection and exploration that each page of this journal would bring about would stimulate new avenues of thought and insights.

So let your child write, sketch, doodle or whatever it takes to give a life to their thoughts. These exciting pages are waiting to be explored and written upon to get permanent impressions from your child.

Happy Journaling!

Notes

Index

Week 1:	Name Thoughts!	9
Week 2:	My Family My World	11
Week 3:	Growing Up Times	13
Week 4:	I am Special	15
Week 5:	Job Watch	17
Week 6:	Caring Gestures	19
Week 7:	Down the Memory Lane	21
Week 8:	How is your Day Like!	23
Week 9:	Give it a Thought	25
Week 10:	Mirror, Mirror on the Wall	27
Week 11:	My Wish List	29
Week 12:	My Choices	31
Week 13:	Round The Clock	33
Week 14:	Best Buddies	35
Week 15:	Look Deeper	37
Week 16:	Welcome To My School	39
Week 17:	Scary Thoughts	41
Week 18:	Book Worms	43
Week 19:	Food Thoughts	45
Week 20:	Play Time	47
Week 21:	Weather Watch	49
Week 22:	Curious Student	51
Week 23:	Stretch your Imagination	53
Week 24:	What's the Question	55
Week 25:	Build It Up	57
Week 26:	Playing With Words	59
Week 27:	Get Set Go	61
Week 28:	Get Inventing	63
Week 29:	Money Wise	65
Week 30:	Holiday Destination	67
Week 31:	Electrifying World	69
Week 32:	Popular Advertisements	71
Week 33:	Shop Till You Drop	73
Week 34:	On The Go	75
Week 35:	I am a Busy Bee	77
Week 36:	Animal Lover	79
Week 37:	Oh! That Can't Be True	81
Week 38:	World of Fairy Tales	83
Week 39:	Super Sports	85
Week 40:	Music and Melody	87
Week 41:	Let's Celebrate	89
Week 42:	Movie Mania	91
Week 43:	Health Talk	93
Week 44:	Helping Hands	95
Week 45:	Computer Geek	97
Week 46:	Nurture the Nature	99
Week 47:	Animal Lover	101
Week 48:	Supercool Superhero	103
Week 49:	Treasure Hunt	105
Week 50:	Sound Sense	107
Week 51:	Surprise	109
Week 52:	Law and Order	111

ALL ABOUT ME - *Journal for kids*

Notes

Name Thoughts!

Week 1

Write an acrostic poem using your name.

Write 5 other names that you like.

ALL ABOUT ME - *Journal for kids*

9

Name Thoughts!

Week 1

How was your name decided upon?

....
....
....
....
....
....

Write about 5 most important things that your family has taught you.

....
....
....
....
....
....
....
....
....
....

ALL ABOUT ME - *Journal for kids*

My Family My World

Week 2

Write about your family. Write a sentence for each member to describe how they are.

....

....

....

....

....

....

....

....

....

....

....

....

....

....

....

....

ALL ABOUT ME - *Journal for kids*

My Family, My World

Week 2

In what ways is your family different than your friend's family?

....
....
....
....
....
....
....
....
....
....
....
....
....

Write different ways people greet and say 'hello' in different languages of the world.

ALL ABOUT ME - *Journal for kids*

12

Growing Up Times

Week 3

How old were you four years ago? Describe some things you can do now that you could not do then.

....

....

....

....

....

....

....

....

....

....

....

....

....

....

Do you remember any baby words that you used to say?

ALL ABOUT ME - *Journal for kids*

Growing Up Times

Write a few things than you can't do now but will be able to do in future.

....

....

....

....

....

....

....

....

....

....

....

....

....

Make a list of a few things that kids like to do.

ALL ABOUT ME - *Journal for kids*

Week 3

14

I am Special

Week 4

Write all the things that you are good at.

....

....

....

....

....

....

Write about all your accomplishments so far. Did you win any contest, awards, any certificates of appreciation?

....

....

....

....

....

....

....

....

ALL ABOUT ME - *Journal for kids*

I am Special

Week 4

What are your hobbies? Do you plan to add any new hobbies in future?

....
....
....
....
....
....
....
....
....
....
....
....
....

List down all the things that your mother is good at.

ALL ABOUT ME - *Journal for kids*

16

Job Watch

Week 5

Describe your father's and mother's job. Even if one of your parents stay at home, they have lots of things at hand. Write all about it!

....
....
....
....
....
....

What would you like to be when you grow up? Explain what would the job require you to do.

....
....
....
....
....
....
....
....

ALL ABOUT ME - *Journal for kids*

17

Job Watch

Week 5

List 10 most important occupations according to you.

....

....

....

....

....

....

....

....

....

....

Do you know the occupation of your any 3 best friend's parents.

ALL ABOUT ME - *Journal for kids*

18

Caring Gestures

Week 6

Write a poem for an important person in your life.

Hallmark Greeting Card Company would be happy to print your poem on a card. Design a nice card to go along.

ALL ABOUT ME - *Journal for kids*

19

Caring Gestures

Week 6

What different things can you do to show love for your family?

....
....
....
....
....
....
....
....
....
....
....
....
....
....

Write a loving note to your mother.

ALL ABOUT ME - *Journal for kids*

20

Down the Memory Lane

Week 7

Prepare a list of all the memorable days of your life.

....
....
....
....
....
....
....
....
....
....

Show these events on a time line.

ALL ABOUT ME - *Journal for kids*

Down the Memory Lane

Week 7

Write about the best gift you ever received. Who gave it to you?

....

....

....

....

....

....

....

Write a list of handmade things that can be given as gifts.

....

....

....

....

....

....

....

....

ALL ABOUT ME - *Journal for kids*

How is your Day Like!

Week 8

Describe a perfect day for you. Put in as many details as you can.
Make it a possible day, not a "dream day."

ALL ABOUT ME - *Journal for kids*

How is your Day Like!

Week 8

The things that get me upset are……

....

....

....

....

....

....

Write 5 things that cheer you up when you feel sad.

....

....

....

....

....

....

....

ALL ABOUT ME - *Journal for kids*

24

Give it a Thought

Week 9

The hardest thing you've ever done.

....
....
....
....
....
....

What is your greatest ambition.

....
....
....
....
....
....
....
....

ALL ABOUT ME - *Journal for kids*

Give it a Thought

Week 9

Write about some of the things that you worry about.

....
....
....
....
....
....
....

I have a complaint.

....
....
....
....
....
....
....

ALL ABOUT ME - *Journal for kids*

26

Mirror, Mirror on the Wall

Week 10

When I take a good look at myself in the mirror this is what I see.

....

....

....

....

....

....

....

....

....

....

....

....

....

....

....

....

ALL ABOUT ME - *Journal for kids*

Mirror, Mirror on the Wall

Week 10

What do you like best about your home?
Which is your most favourite corner in your home? Why?

....

....

....

....

....

Write a list of all the things you have in your room.

....

....

....

....

....

....

....

....

ALL ABOUT ME - *Journal for kids*

My Wish List

Week 11

For my next birthday I wish I could get:

....
....
....
....
....
....
....
....
....
....
....
....
....
....
....
....
....
....
....

ALL ABOUT ME - *Journal for kids*

My Wish List

Week 11

These are 3 things I wish for my family.

....

....

....

....

....

....

Put full stop at the end of the sentence.

....

....

....

....

....

....

....

ALL ABOUT ME - *Journal for kids*

30

My Choices

Week 12

What is your favorite color? Explain why this is your favorite color. List some things that have this color.

....
....
....
....
....
....
....
....
....
....
....
....

List down all the white things in your house.

ALL ABOUT ME - *Journal for kids*

My Choices

Week 12

Your friends want you to throw a fun New Year party. Describe where would you have your party and tell about all the things that you would do.

ALL ABOUT ME - *Journal for kids*

Round The Clock

Week 13

Make a list of your everyday chores; all of them from morning to evening.

....
....
....
....
....
....
....

Sort them into two categories: Interesting/Boring

....
....
....
....
....
....
....

ALL ABOUT ME - *Journal for kids*

33

Round The Clock

Week 13

These are the things I am responsible for at home.

....

....

....

....

....

....

These are the things I am responsible for at school.

Interesting	Boring

ALL ABOUT ME - *Journal for kids*

Best Buddies

Week 14

Write about the qualities that a good friend should have.

....

....

....

....

....

....

....

....

....

....

....

....

....

Write names of all the friends you have made so far.

ALL ABOUT ME - *Journal for kids*

35

Best Buddies

Week 14

Write a thank you note to a friend who was of great help to you.

Look Deeper

Week 15

Choose any one person; it could be your brother, sister, cousin or friend. Describe how are you similar to them?

ALL ABOUT ME - *Journal for kids*

Look Deeper

Week 15

Choose any one person; it could be your brother, sister, cousin or friend. Describe how are you different from them?

Differences .... Similarity

ALL ABOUT ME - *Journal for kids*

Welcome To My School

Week 16

Here's what a new student needs to know about my school.

How old is your school. Who was the first principal?

ALL ABOUT ME - *Journal for kids*

Welcome To My School

Week 16

Write a few things that you would like to change about your school.

What is the motto of your school. Can you draw your school's emblem here?

ALL ABOUT ME - *Journal for kids*

40

Scary Thoughts

Week 17

Write all the things that scare you.

....
....
....
....
....
....
....

These are the things I do when I'm scared.

....
....
....
....
....
....
....
....

ALL ABOUT ME - *Journal for kids*

Scary Thoughts

Week 17

Do you believe in superstitions? What are the common superstitions that people usually believe in?

ALL ABOUT ME - *Journal for kids*

42

Book Worms

Week 18

Write about the best book that you ever read. What did you like about it. Who is the author?

....

....

....

....

....

....

....

....

....

....

....

....

....

Write the names of all the characters that you remember from the books you read.

ALL ABOUT ME - *Journal for kids*

43

Book Worms

Week 18

Write about a favorite character from a book that you read.

....

....

....

....

....

....

Design a new cover page of your favorite book

....

....

....

....

....

....

....

....

ALL ABOUT ME - *Journal for kids*

Food Thoughts

Week 19

What is that one dish that you would like to cook for your friends. Why do you like it so much?

....

....

....

....

....

....

....

Pen down the recipe of your favorite dish.

....

....

....

....

....

....

....

....

ALL ABOUT ME - *Journal for kids*

Food Thoughts

Week 19

Make a list of all your favorite foods.

Your least liked foods.

ALL ABOUT ME - *Journal for kids*

Play Time

Week 20

Write about your favourite childhood toy. Where did you get it from? If that toy could talk to you what would it say?

....

Make a list of all your favorite toys.

ALL ABOUT ME - *Journal for kids*

Play Time

List down all the activities you can do staying indoors to keep yourself occupied when it is raining outside.

....

....

....

....

....

....

....

Make a list of all the outdoor games that you play.

ALL ABOUT ME - *Journal for kids*

Weather Watch

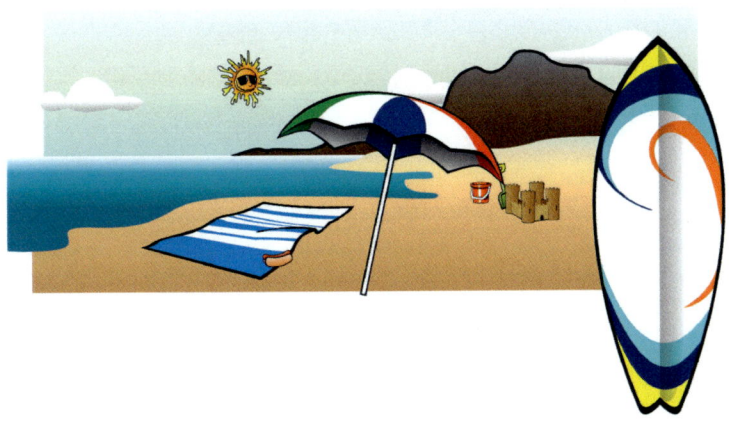

Week 21

...of which is hidden behind the ...icture.

....
....
....
....
....
....
....
....
....
....
....
....
....
....

Make a list of all the things that you get to see or do only during this season.

ALL ABOUT ME - *Journal for kids*

49

Weather Watch

Week 21

You are a kite in the sky flying high on a windy day. Write all the things that you see below. How does it feel to be on top of everything?

ALL ABOUT ME - *Journal for kids*

Curious Student

Week 22

Dear teacher, "I would like to ask you some questions."

....

ALL ABOUT ME - *Journal for kids*

51

Curious Student

Week 22

Write 5 things that you have learnt from your teacher.

....

....

....

....

....

....

....

....

....

....

....

....

....

....

List down names of all your teachers who have taught you so far since your childhood.

ALL ABOUT ME - *Journal for kids*

52

Stretch your Imagination

Week 23

Imagine you could take any 5 objects to a deserted island. What would you take? Explain why you made these choices.

....
....
....
....
....
....
....
....
....
....
....
....
....
....

Make a list of the most expensive things that you know of.

ALL ABOUT ME - *Journal for kids*

Stretch your Imagination

Week 23

Write about what you think life would be like 100 years from now.

ALL ABOUT ME - *Journal for kids*

What's the Question

Week 24

Choose a topic you are interested in. It could be absolutely anything! Write down some questions that you want to know the answers for. Now do your research to answer those.

ALL ABOUT ME - *Journal for kids*

55

What's the Question

Week 24

The answer is 'Blue'.
Write as many questions that you can think of for which the answer is 'Blue'.

ALL ABOUT ME - *Journal for kids*

Build It Up

Week 25

Describe your house to someone who has never seen it.

....
....
....
....
....
....
....
....
....
....
....
....
....
....

Here is a picture of my house.

ALL ABOUT ME - *Journal for kids*

57

Build It Up

Week 25

Write all the steps that you think are needed while building a house.

Make a list of all the materials that can be used to build a house.

ALL ABOUT ME - *Journal for kids*

Playing With Words

Week 26

Make a riddle of your own.
Check if your friends can crack it!

Try out making your own tongue twister. Do share it with your friends.

ALL ABOUT ME - *Journal for kids*

Playing With Words

Week 26

Write any two of your favorite jokes that make you laugh the most.

....

....

....

....

....

Make a list of most funny people you have met so far.

....

....

....

....

....

....

....

....

ALL ABOUT ME - *Journal for kids*

Get Set Go

Week 27

Write all the things that you pack in your suitcase when you travel.

....

....

....

....

....

....

What would Sleeping Beauty pack in her suitcase? Why?

....

....

....

....

....

....

....

....

ALL ABOUT ME - *Journal for kids*

Get Set Go

Week 27

Write about a country you know most about.

....
....
....
....
....
....
....
....
....
....
....
....
....
....

List down all the countries you have visited so far.

ALL ABOUT ME - *Journal for kids*

Get Inventing

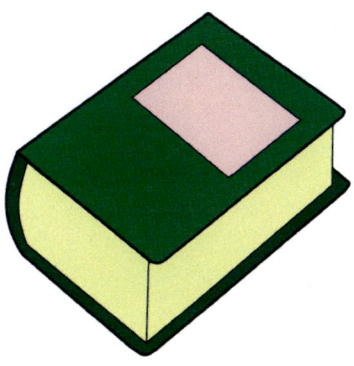

Week 28

If you could invent a new word for the dictionary what would it be? What does it mean? Is it a noun, verb, adjective etc.?

Make a list of longest words you know of. Have you heard of words like **Supercalifragilisticexpialidocious**. It means "Wonderful". Have fun making some of your own and write their meaning.

ALL ABOUT ME - *Journal for kids*

Get Inventing

If you could invent anything what would it be?
What would you name this invention. What can it do?

Week 28

ALL ABOUT ME - *Journal for kids*

Money Wise

Week 29

Look at this $5 note, where has it been until now? Write its story and all the places it went with people.

Make a list of all the things you could buy with $5.

ALL ABOUT ME - *Journal for kids*

Money Wise

Week 29

Describe several ways a person of your age can earn money.

ALL ABOUT ME - *Journal for kids*

Holiday Destination

Week 30

Which is your most favorite place that you have visited so far? Write all the things that you did there. Why do you find it so exciting?

....
....
....
....
....
....
....
....
....
....
....
....
....
....
....
....
....
....

Holiday Destination

Week 30

If you had to escort visitors from another country to show around your country, which all places would you take them to?

ALL ABOUT ME - *Journal for kids*

Electrifying World

Week 31

Write down all the things you couldn't do if there was no electricity.

....
....
....
....
....
....
....
....
....
....
....
....
....

Make a list of all the gadgets in your house that run on electricity.

ALL ABOUT ME - *Journal for kids*

69

Electrifying World

Week 31

Which gadgets were used in the past that are not used in present times at all. To get your thoughts rolling typewriter is one such example.

Popular Advertisements

Week 32

Which commercial on TV do you like beyond all others? What about it interests you?

....
....
....
....
....
....
....
....
....
....
....
....

Write any favorite jingle/slogan of an advertisement you like.

ALL ABOUT ME - *Journal for kids* 71

Popular Advertisements

Week 32

If you were asked to prepare an advertisement to sell this car, what would it say?

ALL ABOUT ME - *Journal for kids*

72

Shop Till You Drop

Week 33

Write about going shopping for new clothes. What kind of clothes do you like to buy?

ALL ABOUT ME - *Journal for kids*

Shop Till You Drop

Week 33

Make a list of as many different kinds of clothes that you can think of.

ALL ABOUT ME - *Journal for kids*

On The Go

Week 34

Observe any 5 things that happen on your way home from school. Write about them.

On The Go

Week 34

A new person in the town wants to go from your home to your school. Can you write directions for him? A rough map would be a great thing to add.

A map to reach my school from my home.

ALL ABOUT ME - *Journal for kids*

76

I am a Busy Bee

Week 35

Write all the things that you do during holidays and weekends.

I am a Busy Bee

Week 35

Write a list of 10 things that happened during this month.

....

....

....

....

....

....

....

....

....

....

Write 10 things you can do in 5 minutes.

ALL ABOUT ME - *Journal for kids*

Animal Lover

Week 36

Which is that animal that you know a lot about. Write down some information about it.

....

....

....

....

....

....

....

....

....

....

....

....

Write 10 words you could use to describe any animal.

ALL ABOUT ME - *Journal for kids*

79

Animal Lover

Write all the ways in which you think we are different from animals.

ALL ABOUT ME - *Journal for kids*

Week 36

Oh! That Can't Be True

Week 37

Make a list of things that are hard to believe.

ALL ABOUT ME - *Journal for kids*

Oh! That Can't Be True

Week 37

Its an amazing world out there. Write down some amazing facts about plants, animals, human beings or the world that we live in.

ALL ABOUT ME - *Journal for kids*

82

World of Fairy Tales

Week 38

Can you write a fairy tale in just five lines? Do read it out to your friend once you are done.

....
....
....
....
....
....
....
....
....
....
....
....
....

List down your favorite fairy Tales.

ALL ABOUT ME - Journal for kids

World of Fairy Tales

Week 38

Let's twist a fairy tale a bit. Change and write a new ending of any of your favorite fairy tale.

ALL ABOUT ME - *Journal for kids*

Super Sports

Week 39

What sports do you like to play? Write the rules of any one game that you play.

Super Sports

Write A to Z words related to sports.

A – Archery

B – Badminton

C –

D –

Music and Melody

Week 40

List down your top 10 favorite songs along with their singers.

....

....

....

....

....

....

....

....

....

....

Pen down all the musical instruments you can think of.

ALL ABOUT ME - *Journal for kids*

Music and Melody

Week 40

Write the lyrics of your favorite song.

Let's Celebrate

Week 41

Which is your most favorite festival? Why? What are some of the customs and traditions followed during the celebration?

....
....
....
....
....
....
....
....
....
....
....
....
....
....
....
....

ALL ABOUT ME - *Journal for kids*

Let's Celebrate

Write a short folk tale associated with your favorite festival.

Movie Mania

Week 42

Which is your favorite movie? Describe the best scene of this movie.

ALL ABOUT ME - *Journal for kids*

91

Movie Mania

Week 42

Make a list of movies you have watched so far.

....

....

....

....

....

....

....

....

....

....

....

....

....

List down names of as many film stars that you know of.

ALL ABOUT ME - *Journal for kids*

Health Talk

Week 43

It is important to eat healthy and exercise.
Write about some different ways to stay healthy.

....

....

....

....

....

....

....

....

....

....

....

....

Make a list of healthy things you eat for your breakfast

ALL ABOUT ME - *Journal for kids*

Health Talk

Week 43

If you had an entire garden, write about some of the things that you would plant in your garden.

....
....
....
....
....
....

In what ways will you take care of your garden.

....
....
....
....
....
....

ALL ABOUT ME - *Journal for kids*

Helping Hands

Week 44

Write about some things you should always do to be a good citizen.

ALL ABOUT ME - *Journal for kids*

Helping Hands

Week 44

Imagine that someone gave you 1 Million Dollars. Write 10 ways you could give that money to needy people.

ALL ABOUT ME - *Journal for kids*

Computer Geek

Week 45

A computer can be used in so many ways. What are your favorite thing to do on the computer.

ALL ABOUT ME - *Journal for kids*

97

Computer Geek

Week 45

If you could create your own website, what would it be about? What would it be called? How would you use it to help others?

....
....
....
....
....

List down the favorite websites that you visit.

....
....
....
....
....
....
....
....

ALL ABOUT ME - *Journal for kids*

Nurture the Nature

Week 46

Think about our amazing planet Earth. Write about different ways in which we can help protect our planet.

....
....
....
....
....
....
....
....
....
....
....
....
....
....
....

ALL ABOUT ME - *Journal for kids*

Animal Lover

Week 47

Which is your favorite pet? Write all the things that you need to do to take care of your pet?

....

....

....

....

....

....

....

....

....

....

....

....

....

Make a list of animals that can be kept as pets.

ALL ABOUT ME - *Journal for kids* 101

Animal Lover

Week 47

Which is your favorite pet? Write all the things that you need to do to take care of your pet?

....

....

....

....

....

....

....

Make a list of animals that can be kept as pets.

....

....

....

....

....

....

....

....

ALL ABOUT ME - *Journal for kids*

Animal Lover

Week 47

Imagine if you were a zebra. Would you rather live at a zoo or in the wild? Explain why?

....
....
....
....
....
....
....
....
....
....
....
....
....
....
....

ALL ABOUT ME - *Journal for kids*

Supercool Superhero

Week 48

Imagine that you are a superhero. Write about your super powers and then draw a picture showing how you look like.

....
....
....
....
....
....
....
....
....
....
....
....
....
....

This is how my superhero looks like.

ALL ABOUT ME - *Journal for kids*

Supercool Superhero

Who is your favorite hero? It could be a fiction hero like Superman or it could be a movie star. What qualities in him impress you?

....

....

....

....

....

Write two questions you would ask if you meet your favorite hero?

....

....

....

....

....

....

ALL ABOUT ME - *Journal for kids*

Treasure Hunt

Week 49

One person's trash could be another person's treasure. Write about some treasures that you found in a garage sale or somewhere else.

If you open the dustbin of your house now, what ten things would you find inside?

ALL ABOUT ME - *Journal for kids*

Treasure Hunt

Week 49

Think about all of the things in your house that you have not used since a few months. List some of your things that you would want to donate to families in need.

ALL ABOUT ME - *Journal for kids*

Sound Sense

Week 50

Write about all the different sounds that you hear when you go for a casual walk.

ALL ABOUT ME - *Journal for kids*

Sound Sense

List down as many sound words that you know of. See a few examples to start thinking.
Atchoo – Hee-haw – Oink – jingle

Week 50

ALL ABOUT ME - *Journal for kids*

Surprise....

Week 51

Write about the biggest surprise you ever got.

Write anything that you are excited about this year?

ALL ABOUT ME - *Journal for kids*

Surprise....

Week 51

Write about an April fool prank that you can play on your friend.

ALL ABOUT ME - *Journal for kids*

Law and Order

Week 52

Imagine that you were made the President of your country. Write about a law that you would want to have to help the people in your community.

List down places that are unsafe for you to go alone.

ALL ABOUT ME - *Journal for kids*

Law and Order

Week 52

Write about some of the rules that you follow at school to keep it functioning well.

ALL ABOUT ME - *Journal for kids*

112

Notes

Notes

Made in the USA
Columbia, SC
20 November 2018